Saint-Saëns's Danse Macabre

Anna Harwell Celenza

Illustrated by JoAnn E. Kitchel

ini Charlesbridge

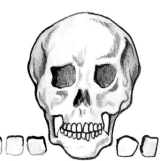

Published by Charlesbridge
85 Main Street
Watertown, MA 02472
(617) 926-0329
www.charlesbridge.com

Library of Congress Cataloging-in-Publication Data
Celenza, Anna Harwell.
   Saint-Saëns's Danse Macabre / Anna Harwell Celenza; illustrated by JoAnn E. Kitchel.
     p. cm.
   ISBN 978-1-57091-348-8 (reinforced for library use)
   ISBN 978-1-60734-612-8 (ebook)
1. Saint-Saëns, Camille, 1835–1921. Danse macabre (Symphonic poem)—Juvenile literature.
2. Saint-Saëns, Camille, 1835–1921—Juvenile literature. 3. Composers—France—Juvenile
literature. I. Kitchel, JoAnn E., ill. II. Title.
ML3930.S15C35 2013
784.2'1843—dc23   2012024575

Printed in Singapore
(hc) 10 9 8 7 6 5 4 3 2 1

Illustrations done in watercolor on Arches hot-press watercolor paper
Display type set in Letterhead Fancy by Billy Jacobs
Text type set in Adobe Caslon Pro by Adobe Systems Incorporated
Color separations by KHL Chroma Graphics, Singapore
Printed and bound February 2013 by Imago in Singapore
Production supervision by Brian G. Walker
Designed by Diane M. Earley

For Dad—my favorite Halloween skeleton
—A. H. C.

For Arianna and her two pianos
—J. E. K.

Deep below the streets of Paris stretch the city's catacombs. Six million skeletons rest peacefully in this underground cemetery. Bones of every shape and size line the damp, stone walls.

On a dark autumn night in 1872, the composer Camille Saint-Saëns and his poet friend Henri Cazalis embarked on a spooky expedition. In search of inspiration, they descended the eighty-three steps that spiral into this chilling ossuary.

"Look!" said Camille as they crept along a tunnel. "The flickering candlelight makes the bones appear to dance."

Henri picked up a pair of thigh bones. "You mean like this?" His voice echoed through the caverns and tunnels. He began to dance a jig.

"Put those down!" said Camille.

"Perhaps you would prefer a haunting melody?" asked Henri. He held the bones like a violin. "Let me tell you a story about Maestro Death. . . ."

Zig and zig and zig. Maestro Death keeps time.
Tapping his heel on a tomb.
Zig and zig and zag on his violin.
At midnight he plays a dancing tune. . . .

A chill ran down Camille's back. "Have you no respect for the dead?" he said.

"Certainly," said Henri. "Among these bones lie the remains of heroes—brave souls who fought in the French Revolution." Henri raised his fist in the air. "Long live equality! Long live death!"

Camille grabbed the bones from Henri and put them back along the wall. "I don't think this is what the revolutionaries had in mind when they stormed the Bastille."

"Maybe not," said Henri, picking up a skull. "But everyone is equal down here. Banker or beggar, all bones look the same."

Camille raised the lantern high and looked down the long tunnel of bones. "Imagine if they suddenly came to life!"

For weeks Camille was haunted by his visit to the catacombs. *Zig and zig and zig. Maestro Death keeps time.* Determined to compose a spine-chilling song, he visited Henri and asked for a copy of his poem.

"But I thought you disapproved," said Henri. "Disrespectful, isn't that what you said?"

"Yes," admitted Camille. "But since then I've changed my mind. I can't stop thinking of dancing skeletons. I want to try to capture that sensation in music."

"Marvelous!" said Henri. He took out a pen and paper and began writing down the words. "I recited only the beginning of the poem in the catacombs," he said. "I'll give you the whole thing now."

With the poem in hand, Camille returned home.
He set Henri's words to music in just a few days. Eager
to learn what his friends thought of the song, he took a
copy with him to a dinner party hosted by Augusta
Holmès, a composer and a marvelous singer.

After dessert Camille, Augusta, and Henri gathered
around the piano. Camille asked Augusta to sing his
new song.

"I'd love to," she said. "Just give me a moment to read
through the words."

When Augusta was ready, Camille played a short
introduction on the piano. Augusta sang Camille's
composition with great passion and emotion.

"No, no, no!" said Camille at the end of the performance. "Augusta, you're singing too amorously. My music is about skeletons rising from the grave."

"But Henri's text mentions a pair of lovers," said Augusta.

"Forget the lovers; they're not important," replied Camille.

Henri protested: "What do you mean they're not important?"

Camille threw his hands in the air. "I give up! Sing the song however you wish. I'm going home."

Several weeks later Camille ran into Augusta at a café.

"I'm sorry I was rude at your dinner party," said Camille.

"I forgive you," said Augusta. "You were upset about my interpretation of your song."

"When I composed the piece, I was thinking about rambunctious skeletons dancing in the moonlight," said Camille. "I never imagined anyone could turn it into a love song."

"That's the difficult thing about being a composer," said Augusta. "Once the music is written, you have to let it go. The performer is the one who brings it to life."

On his way home Camille thought about what Augusta had said. "How can I make sure the audience hears my intentions?" he asked himself. He walked through the Tuileries Garden toward the river. "I must rewrite my music so there is no mistaking what I want. Henri's poem just gets in the way. What I want is skeletons!" Camille raised his fist in the air. "No more singers! No more words!" he shouted. "I will rewrite my *Danse macabre* for instruments alone!"

Camille worked on his composition for nearly two years, carefully marking in the score every musical effect he wanted. He indicated precisely how each note should be played. In his quest for spooky sounds, he mixed waltzes with funeral tunes and experimented with various instruments.

When the masterpiece was finished, Camille invited his friends over for a visit. With excitement he described his composition.

"I wanted to capture the rasp and jangle of waltzing skeletons," he told Henri. "That's why I added a xylophone to the orchestra."

"What about the violins?" asked Augusta. "They don't rattle and clack like skeletons."

"The violins do what I tell them to," said Camille. He showed her a page in the score. "In this section the musicians smack the strings with the wood of the bow. *CLACK, clicky, clicky, CLACK, clicky, clicky, CLACK.*"

"What about Maestro Death?" said Henri. "Does he do as you say?"

"With pleasure," said Camille. "I've given him a diabolical fiddle."

On January 24, 1875, more than two thousand people gathered in the Châtelet Theater to hear Camille's *Danse macabre*.

Dong, dong, dong, dong . . . Twelve strokes of midnight rang out from the harp. The first violinist walked on stage, flashing the audience a devilish grin. He tuned his diabolical fiddle, evoking Maestro Death. Like a shrouded specter, a lilting melody floated up from the orchestra.

One by one the skeletons rose from their graves. Bone against bone, they rattled and danced. The cellos strained. The woodwinds pranced. The xylophone clinked with each step. Fiddle bows clacked to the skeleton dance, spinning and swirling, swooshing and swaying. *Zig and zig and zig.* The boney revelers delighted as Death's fiddle played on.

Through the gloom, skipping bones glowed white. Round and round, they multiplied.

Cloaked in darkness, Death played a funereal waltz. Trombones blasted and cymbals crashed. Jumping and soaring, the skeletons flew.

The oboe played a rooster's cry. Sunlight touched the horizon. Timpani rumbled low in the distance. *Zig and zig and zag*, Maestro Death ended the dance. *Click clack.* Camille's skeletons scampered away.

A heavy silence hung over the concert hall. No one in the audience knew what to make of Camille's music. A few people clapped. Others shouted insults.

"Scandalous!"

"Pure nonsense."

"Horrific!"

Camille walked onstage and took a deep bow. His friends looked worried, but there was no need. Camille didn't care what the audience thought. The orchestra had played his *Danse macabre* just the way he wanted it. His ghoulish skeletons had finally come to life. Camille imagined them applauding from the catacombs. . . .

"Bravo!" cheered the bones. "Long live the music!
Long live the dance!"

Author's Note

Based on historical fact, this book tells the story behind *Danse macabre* by Camille Saint-Saëns (1835–1921). Inspiration for this symphonic poem came from the Paris Catacombs, which were created in 1786, when bones from overcrowded cemeteries were transferred to abandoned limestone quarries below the city's streets. A decade later, victims of the French Revolution were buried there, followed in 1871 by insurgents who were killed during another uprising: the "Bloody Week" of the Paris Commune.

Throughout the nineteenth century, curious thrill seekers ventured into the catacombs by candlelight. Henri Cazalis (1840–1909) was among them, and in 1868 he published a poem inspired by his visit, titled "Equality, Brotherhood," which describes death as society's great equalizer. Saint-Saëns surely visited the catacombs. He likely didn't accompany Cazalis, but he did use his friend's poem as the text for his song "Danse macabre." (The French word *macabre* likely comes from the Arabic word *maqābir*, which means "cemeteries," or the Hebrew word מהקבר, pronounced "Mehakever," meaning "from the grave.")

In its first public performance, "Danse macabre" was sung by Augusta Holmès (1847–1903), a composer who made a strong impression on Parisian society with her intelligence and beauty. Reviews of the concert praised Holmès's performance but dismissed the music. Saint-Saëns responded by rewriting the piece for orchestra alone.

In his revision Saint-Saëns eliminated all references to politics and turned the traditional funeral chant *Dies Irae* into a dance. To evoke Death's "diabolical fiddle," he instructed the first violinist to tune the E string a half step lower, thus creating a dissonant interval—the tritone, nicknamed *diabolus in musica* (the devil in music). For the rattling bones he instructed the other violinists to play *col legno*, or "with the wood" of their bows. He also added a xylophone, an instrument so new to the orchestra that he wrote in the score where one could be purchased. Later, he used the xylophone again in the "Fossils" movement of his *Carnival of the Animals*.

Saint-Saëns had a sarcastic sense of humor. "I am an eclectic spirit," he once admitted. Although critics rejected *Danse macabre* after the premiere, Saint-Saëns had the last laugh when the composition became one of his most popular works. On April 1, 1897, fifty musicians descended into the Paris Catacombs and performed *Danse macabre*. I can only imagine the bones enjoyed it!